A CHRISTMAS CAROL

Ebenezer Scrooge is a cross, miserable, mean old man. When his nephew visits him on Christmas Eve to wish him a merry Christmas, Scrooge is not at all pleased. 'Bah! Humbug!' he says. 'Christmas is humbug! Everyone who goes around saying "Merry Christmas" should have his tongue cut out. Yes, he should!'

Oh yes, Scrooge is a hard, mean man. His clerk, Bob Cratchit, gets only fifteen shillings a week, and has to work in a cold little office, with a fire too small to warm even his toes.

But that Christmas Eve Scrooge is visited by the ghost of his long-dead partner, Jacob Marley. And after him come three more ghostly visitors . . . It is a long night, and a frightening night, and when Christmas Day finally arrives, Scrooge is a very different man indeed.

OXFORD BOOKWORMS LIBRARY
Classics

A Christmas Carol

Stage 3 (1000 headwords)

Series Editor: Jennifer Bassett
Founder Editor: Tricia Hedge
Activities Editors: Jennifer Bassett and Alison Baxter

CHARLES DICKENS

A Christmas Carol

Retold by
Clare West

Illustrated by
Ian Miller

OXFORD UNIVERSITY PRESS

OXFORD
UNIVERSITY PRESS

Great Clarendon Street, Oxford OX2 6DP

Oxford University Press is a department of the University of Oxford
It furthers the University's objective of excellence in research, scholarship,
and education by publishing worldwide in

Oxford New York

Auckland Bangkok Buenos Aires Cape Town Chennai
Dar es Salaam Delhi Hong Kong Istanbul Karachi Kolkata
Kuala Lumpur Madrid Melbourne Mexico City Mumbai Nairobi
São Paulo Shanghai Taipei Tokyo Toronto

Oxford and Oxford English are registered trade marks of
Oxford University Press in the UK and in certain other countries

ISBN 0 19 4230007 7

This simplified edition © Oxford University Press 2000

Ninth impression 2003

First published in Oxford Bookworms 1996
This second edition published in the Oxford Bookworms Library 2000

A complete recording of this Bookworms edition of *A Christmas Carol*
is available on cassette ISBN 0 19 422881 9

Typeset by Wyvern Typesetting Ltd, Bristol
Printed in Spain by Unigraf s.l.

CONTENTS

1

Marley's ghost

It is important to remember that Jacob Marley was dead. Did Scrooge know that? Of course he did. Scrooge and Marley had been partners in London for many years, and excellent men of business they were, too. When Marley died, Scrooge continued with the business alone. Both names still stood above the office door: Scrooge and Marley. Sometimes people who were new to the business called Scrooge Scrooge, and sometimes Marley, but he

Both names still stood above the office door.

answered to both names. He did not care what name they called him. The only thing that mattered to him was the business, and making money.

Oh! He was a hard, clever, mean old man, Scrooge was! There was nothing warm or open about him. He lived a secretive, lonely life, and took no interest in other people at all. The cold inside him made his eyes red, and his thin lips blue, and his voice high and cross. It put white frost on his old head, his eyebrows and his chin. The frost in his heart made the air around him cold, too. In the hottest days of summer his office was as cold as ice, and it was just as cold in winter.

Nobody ever stopped him in the street to say, with a happy smile, 'My dear Scrooge, how are you? When will

The cold put white frost on his head, his eyebrows and his chin.

you come to see me?' No poor man asked him for money, no children asked him the time, no man or woman ever, in all his life, asked him the way. Animals as well as people were afraid of him. Dogs used to hide in doorways when they saw him coming. But what did Scrooge care! It was just what he wanted. He liked being on the edge of people's busy lives, while warning everyone to keep away from him.

One Christmas Eve, old Scrooge was working busily in his office. It was cold, frosty, foggy weather. Outside it was already dark, although it was only three o'clock in the afternoon, and there were candles in all the office windows. The fog covered everything, like a thick grey blanket.

Scrooge kept his office door open, in order to check that his clerk, Bob Cratchit, was working. Bob spent his days in a dark little room, a kind of cupboard, next to his employer's office. Scrooge had a very small fire, but Bob's fire was much smaller. It was very cold in the cupboard, and Bob had to wear his long white scarf to try to keep warm.

'Merry Christmas, uncle! God bless you!' cried a happy voice. Scrooge's nephew had arrived.

'Bah!' said Scrooge crossly. 'Humbug!'

'Christmas is humbug! Surely you don't mean that, uncle?' said his nephew.

'I do,' said Scrooge. 'Why do you call it "merry" Christmas? You're too poor to be merry.'

3

'Well,' replied the nephew, smiling, 'why are you so cross? You're too rich to be unhappy.'

'Of course I'm cross,' answered the uncle, 'when I live in a world full of stupid people like you! You say "Merry Christmas"! But what is Christmas? Just a time when you spend too much, when you find yourself a year older and not an hour richer, when you have to pay your bills.

Scrooge kept his door open to check that Bob Cratchit was working.

Everyone who goes around saying "Merry Christmas" should have his tongue cut out. Yes, he should!'

'Uncle! Please don't say that!' said the nephew. 'I've always thought of Christmas as a time to be helpful and kind to other people. It's the only time of the year when men and women open their hearts freely to each other. And so, uncle, although I've never made any money from it, I think Christmas has been and will be a good time for me! And I say, God bless Christmas!'

Bob, in the cupboard, agreed loudly, without thinking. He immediately realized his mistake, and went quickly back to his work, but Scrooge had heard him.

'If I hear another sound from *you*,' said Scrooge, 'you'll lose your job!'

'Don't be angry with him, uncle,' said the nephew. 'Come and have dinner with us tomorrow.'

'Dinner with you? I'll see you dead first!'

'But why won't you come? Why?'

'Because Christmas is humbug! Good afternoon!'

'I want nothing from you. I ask nothing of you. Why can't we be friends?'

'Good afternoon!' said Scrooge.

'I am sorry, with all my heart, to find you like this. I have never wanted to argue with you. But I came to see you and invite you because it's Christmas, and so I'll say, a merry Christmas, uncle!'

'Good afternoon,' said Scrooge.

'And a happy new year!'

'Good afternoon!' said Scrooge.

His nephew left the room, without an angry word, stopping only to wish Bob Cratchit a merry Christmas.

Then two other gentlemen came in. They were large, round, comfortable-looking men, with books and papers in their hands.

'This is Scrooge and Marley's, I think,' said one of them, looking at the papers that he was carrying. 'Am I speaking to Mr Scrooge or Mr Marley?'

'Mr Marley is dead,' Scrooge replied. 'He died seven years ago today, on Christmas Eve.'

'I'm sure that you are just as kind to the poor as your partner,' said the gentleman, smiling.

What *was* true was that Scrooge was just as mean as Marley, and Marley had been just as mean as Scrooge.

'At this happy time of year, Mr Scrooge,' the gentleman went on, taking up his pen, 'we should help poor people who have no food or clothes or homes.'

'Are there no prisons?' asked Scrooge coldly.

'Plenty of prisons,' said the gentleman.

'And the workhouses, where poor people can live and work? Are they still open?'

'Yes, they are, I'm sorry to say.'

'I'm happy to hear it,' said Scrooge. 'I thought, from what you said at first, that perhaps these useful places were closed, for some reason.'

'But some of us feel,' replied the gentleman, 'that these places don't offer enough to poor people. We're hoping to

6

give some meat and drink, and wood for a fire, to people who need all these things. This is a time when we should all be able to enjoy ourselves. How much will you give, sir?'

'Nothing!' Scrooge replied. 'I don't have a merry Christmas myself, and I won't pay for other people to be merry. We all have to pay for prisons and workhouses – they cost enough. The poor will have to go there.'

'Many can't go there, and many prefer to die.'

'If they prefer to die, why don't they die, then? There are too many people in the world, so it's a good thing if some of them die. All this is none of my business! It's enough for a man to understand his own business, and not to think about other people's. I'm a very busy man. Good afternoon, gentlemen!'

The gentlemen shook their heads a little sadly, and left the office. Scrooge went back to his work, feeling pleased with himself.

Now the fog was at its thickest outside, and the cold was biting. Lights shone brightly from the shop windows. People were hurrying here and there – rich and poor alike – to buy what they needed for tomorrow's Christmas dinner.

At last it was time to close the office. Scrooge got up slowly from his desk. Bob was waiting for this moment, and he immediately put on his hat.

'You'll want a holiday all day tomorrow, I suppose?' said Scrooge.

7

'If you don't mind, sir.'

'I *do* mind. It's not fair. I have to pay you for a day's work when you don't *do* any work.'

'It's only once a year, sir,' said Bob politely.

'That's no reason for robbing me every twenty-fifth of December!' said Scrooge, putting on his coat. 'But I suppose you must have it. Be here early next morning.'

'Yes, sir, I will, I promise,' Bob said happily. Scrooge walked out, without another word. When Bob had closed the office, he ran home to his family in Camden Town as quickly as possible.

Scrooge always used to eat his dinner alone, in the same miserable little eating-house. Tonight was no different from other nights. He read the newspapers, looked at his bank books, and went home to bed. He lived in rooms which had once belonged to his dead partner. They were in an old, dark building in a lonely side street, where no one except Scrooge lived.

In the blackness of the night, through the fog and the frost, Scrooge had to feel his way along the street with his hands. He finally reached his front door and put the key in the lock. Suddenly, to his great surprise, he saw that the knocker was not a knocker any more, but had become the face of Jacob Marley!

He had not thought of his partner for seven years, until that afternoon, when he spoke Marley's name to his visitors. But there in front of him was Marley's face, white and ghostly, with terrible staring eyes.

The knocker had become the face of Jacob Marley!

As Scrooge looked, it became a knocker again. He was afraid, but he did not show his fear. He turned the key, opened the door and walked in. He *did* look around before

9

he shut the door, and he *did* look behind the door, to see if anyone was hiding there. But there was nothing there. He shut the door with a bang, to show that he was not afraid.

With his one candle he went slowly up the stairs. It was impossible to see into all the dark corners. Darkness was cheap, and Scrooge liked it. But he remembered the face, so he walked through all his rooms, checking that everything was all right. Nobody under the table or the bed, nobody behind the door! On the small fire in the bedroom there was a pot of soup, and Scrooge's bowl was ready on the table. Nobody in any of the rooms! Sure that he was safe now, Scrooge shut and locked his bedroom door behind him. He sat down by the fire to eat his soup.

The fireplace was an old one, with hundreds of pictures on the tiles around the fire. But Scrooge could only see Marley's face on every tile.

'Humbug!' said Scrooge to the tiles, and walked across the room. When he sat down again, he noticed a bell on the other side of the room. As he looked, he saw, with great surprise and fear, that the bell

The fireplace was an old one.

was slowly beginning to move from side to side. Soon it was ringing loudly, and so was every bell in the house.

Suddenly they all stopped ringing at the same moment, and then came a strange noise from down below. It sounded like someone pulling heavy chains across the floor. Scrooge remembered hearing that ghosts in old houses sometimes pulled chains behind them. Then a door below opened with a crash, and the noise started coming up the stairs. It was coming towards his door.

'It's humbug still!' cried Scrooge. But the colour left his face when, without stopping, it came straight through the heavy, locked door, and appeared in front of him. It was Marley's ghost!

Scrooge could see right through its body. Around its middle was a long chain, which had money-boxes, keys, bank books, and heavy purses on it. The ghost's death-cold eyes stared fixedly at Scrooge.

'Well!' said Scrooge, trying to pretend that nothing strange was happening. 'What do y*ou* want? And who are you?'

'In life I was your partner, Jacob Marley.'

'It's humbug, I tell you!' said Scrooge. 'There *are* no ghosts!' But when he said this, the ghost gave a terrible cry, and shook its chain in a very frightening way. At once Scrooge fell on the ground in great fear, crying, 'Yes! Yes! You *are* real! I see that now! Why have you come? Why do ghosts come back from the dead? Tell me, Jacob!'

'The spirit of every man who does not help other people

11

in life has to travel endlessly through the world after his death. We have to carry the chains that we made for ourselves in our lifetime. Do you, Ebenezer Scrooge, recognize my chain? It is very like the one that you wear!'

Scrooge looked around him, but could see no chain. 'Jacob,' he said, 'please tell me more!'

'I cannot help you much, Ebenezer! I cannot rest, I cannot stay anywhere for long. I have been dead for seven years and all that time I have been travelling on the wings of the wind! No peace, no rest for me in death, because I was never good or kind in life!'

'But you were always a good man of business, Jacob,' said Scrooge, who was now beginning to worry about his own life.

'Business!' cried the ghost miserably. 'Why didn't I think of *people* as my business? I thought only about making money, not about being kind and helpful to other people. Listen to me, Ebenezer! I am here tonight to warn you. You still have a chance to save yourself from what has happened to me. Three spirits will come to visit you: the first tomorrow at one o'clock, the second at the same time the next night, and the third at midnight the following night. You will not see me any more, and for your own peace after death, remember what I have told you!'

The spirit walked slowly backwards to the window, which began to open. When the ghost reached the window, it held up its hand, and Scrooge listened. He could hear a noise of sad crying in the air. The spirit began to cry, too,

'Do you, Ebenezer Scrooge, recognize my chain?'

and it moved out into the frosty, dark night to join the others. Scrooge ran to the window. Outside, the air was full of spirits, all wearing chains like Marley's ghost, all crying miserably as they realized, too late, the terrible mistakes that they had made in their lives.

Little by little, the spirits and their voices disappeared into the fog and the darkness, and the night was silent again. Scrooge closed the window, and checked his bedroom door. It was still locked. He started to say, 'Humbug!' but stopped suddenly. Perhaps because he was very tired, or because it was late, he went straight to bed, without taking off his clothes, and fell asleep immediately.

2

The first of the three spirits

When Scrooge woke up, it was very dark in the room. He heard the church clock start striking, and listened to see what the time was. To his great surprise, the heavy bell went on striking up to twelve, then stopped. Twelve o'clock! It was past two in the morning when he had gone to bed. The clock must be wrong! He looked at his watch. It said twelve o'clock too!

'Have I slept all day? Is it the next night already?' Scrooge asked himself. 'Or has something happened to the sun? Perhaps it's midday, not midnight! But that's impossible!'

He climbed out of bed, and felt his way to the window. But there was nobody outside in the dark, foggy streets, and he realized it must be night-time. He went back to bed again, but could not sleep. He was worried, because he could not understand what was happening. 'Was Marley's ghost a dream?' he wondered. 'But it *seemed* very real . . .'

He lay awake until he heard the clock striking a quarter to the hour. Suddenly he remembered. The ghost had warned him that a spirit would visit him at one o'clock.

14

He decided to stay awake until one o'clock had passed. The quarter of an hour passed very slowly, but at last he heard the clock striking the four quarters.

'It's one o'clock!' cried Scrooge delightedly, 'and nothing has happened!' But he spoke before the hour bell had sounded. The clock now struck a deep, sad ONE, and immediately light shone into Scrooge's bedroom. The curtains round his bed were pulled open. Scrooge sat up in bed, and stared at his ghostly visitor.

A strange figure, half like a child, half like an old man, looked back at him. It had long, white hair, but its skin was soft and young. It wore a short, white robe, covered with both summer and winter flowers. But the strangest thing about it was that from the top of its head shone a bright, clear light. Perhaps this light was sometimes too bright, because under one arm it carried a hat, which looked like a large extinguisher.

'Who and what are you, sir?' asked Scrooge.

'I am the ghost of Christmas Past,' replied the spirit, in a soft, gentle voice.

'Do you mean long ago in the past?' asked Scrooge.

'No. *Your* past.'

'Spirit, please tell me why you are here.'

'I am here for your own good,' answered the ghost.

'Thank you,' replied Scrooge politely. But secretly he thought, 'Bah! A night of unbroken sleep is a more useful thing to have!'

The spirit seemed to hear him thinking, and said at once,

Scrooge stared at his ghostly visitor.

'I am here to help you change your life! Watch and listen!' It put out a strong hand, and held Scrooge by the arm. 'Get up, and come with me!'

It was dark and cold outside. Scrooge did not want to go anywhere, and for a moment he thought about pretending to be too ill to go out. But he did not like to refuse, so he said nothing, and got out of bed. Together they passed through the wall of the house out into the darkness.

Suddenly Scrooge realized they were standing on an open country road, with fields on each side. London, the fog, and the darkness had all disappeared, and it was a clear, cold, winter day, with snow on the ground.

'Good Heavens!' cried Scrooge. 'I was born near here! I remember it well!'

The spirit looked kindly at the old man. 'How strange that you've forgotten it for so many years! What is that on your face? Are you crying?'

Scrooge put a hand over his eyes. 'It's nothing – I've got a cold, that's all. Take me where you want, spirit!'

Scrooge recognized every field, post, and tree, as they walked along the road towards a little market town. All around them were young schoolboys on horses and in farmers' carts, laughing and wishing each other a merry Christmas, as they travelled to their homes for the Christmas holiday.

'They are only shadows from the past,' said the spirit. 'They cannot see us.'

Scrooge knew and named all of them. Why was he so

17

All around them were young schoolboys on horses and in carts.

delighted to see them? Why did his cold heart beat faster
when they went past, shouting 'Merry Christmas!'? What
was 'merry Christmas' to Scrooge? What good had it ever
done to him?

'Not everyone has left the school,' said the ghost. 'There
is one lonely child there still, one child whose friends have
all gone.'

'I know!' said Scrooge. And now he was crying openly.

They turned into a smaller road, and soon came to the
school. Inside, in the long, cold, silent classroom, a lonely
boy sat reading near a small fire. When he saw his poor
forgotten past self, Scrooge sat down at one of the desks,
put his head in his hands and cried.

'Poor boy! I wish – but it's too late now.'

'What's the matter?' asked the spirit.

'There was a boy singing Christmas carols at my door

yesterday. I'm sorry I didn't give him anything, that's all.'

The ghost smiled, and lifted its hand, saying, 'Let's see another past Christmas!'

The schoolroom became darker and dirtier. There was the young Scrooge again, a little older and bigger than before. He was not reading this time, but was walking up and down, looking very unhappy. The door opened, and a little girl, much younger than him, came running in. Putting her arms round his neck, she said lovingly to him, 'I've come to bring you home, dear brother! Father is so much kinder than he used to be! The other day I asked him if you could come home, and he said yes! And we're going to spend Christmas together, and have the merriest time!' She was laughing delightedly as she began to pull him towards the door. They went out happily together, hand in hand.

'What a warm heart she had!' said the ghost.

'You're right,' said Scrooge. 'I agree with you, spirit!'

'She married, I understand,' continued the ghost, 'and had children, I think, before she died.'

'One child,' answered Scrooge.

'True,' said the ghost. 'Your nephew!'

Scrooge did not answer at once. 'Yes,' he said at last.

Now the school had disappeared, and they were in the middle of a busy town, with shadowy crowds and carts all around them. Here it was Christmas time again, but it was evening, and there were lights in the shops and streets.

The ghost stopped at an office door. 'Do you know this place, Scrooge?' he asked.

19

'Know it!' cried Scrooge. 'Why, I was a clerk here!'

They went in, and when they saw a large, kind-looking old gentleman sitting at a high desk, Scrooge cried excitedly, 'Good Heavens, it's old Fezziwig! God bless him! It's Fezziwig alive again!'

Old Fezziwig put down his pen, and looked at the clock. Fastening his coat buttons over his fat stomach, he started laughing as he called out in a rich, deep, happy voice, 'Ebenezer! Dick! Seven o'clock! No more work tonight! It's Christmas Eve, remember!'

The young Scrooge hurried in, with another clerk.

'That's Dick Wilkins!' said Scrooge quietly to the ghost. 'He always liked me. Oh dear! Poor Dick!'

Together the two young clerks put away all the pens and papers, and, following Fezziwig's orders, cleared all

Away they all went in the dance.

the furniture away from the centre of the room. In came a
fiddler. In came Mrs Fezziwig, fat and smiling. In came
the three Fezziwig daughters, sweet and pretty. In came
the six young men who were in love with them. In came
the cook, with her young man, the milkman. In came the
boy from next door, with the girl from the house opposite.
In they came, some quietly, some noisily, but all happy
because it was Christmas Eve. The fiddler started playing,
and away they all went in the dance, twenty pairs at the
same time, round and round, down the middle and up
again. When they were all tired, old Fezziwig cried out,
'Well done! Now, have something to eat and drink!' There
was cake and hot meat and bread and cold meat and fruit,
and all kinds of drinks, on a long table near the door. And
after they had eaten, they danced again.

21

When the clock struck eleven, the dancing ended. Mr and Mrs Fezziwig stood by the door, shaking hands with each person as he or she went out, and wishing him or her a merry Christmas.

During this time Scrooge had thought of nothing except what was happening in front of his eyes. He remembered and enjoyed it all with the greatest delight. But when the dancing came to an end, he realized that the ghost was looking at him. The light on the spirit's head was burning very clearly.

'It seems easy enough to amuse these childish people,' said the ghost. 'It was nothing much that Fezziwig did, was it? After all, he only spent a few pounds, on food and drink and paying the fiddler.'

'It isn't a question of money,' replied Scrooge warmly. He was speaking like the young man he used to be, not the old man he was now. 'No, spirit, you see, our employer can make us happy or sad. His words, his looks, all these things are so important! The happiness that he gives is just as valuable as money!'

He suddenly stopped speaking, when he felt the spirit watching him closely.

'What's the matter?' asked the ghost.

'Er – nothing,' said Scrooge. 'Just that – I'd like to be able to say a word or two to my clerk now.'

Now Scrooge could see himself again. He was older now, and it was clear that he was beginning to show an unhealthy interest in money. His eyes were restless, and his mouth looked thin and mean. He was not alone, but was sitting beside a lovely young girl. The light that shone brightly from the ghost of Christmas Past showed that she was crying.

'I know it doesn't matter very much to *you*,' she said softly. 'You care about gold more than you care about me. Perhaps I shouldn't be sad. Money will give you the happiness that *I* wanted to give you.'

'But I haven't changed towards you, have I?'

'You *have* changed. We promised to marry a long time ago, when we were both poor, and happy to be poor. I have stayed the same, but you have different hopes and dreams now. I loved the man that you used to be, but I know that you do not wish to marry me any more. So I've come to tell you that you're free. Be happy in the life that you've chosen!' And she left him.

'Spirit!' cried Scrooge. 'Show me no more! Take me home! This is too painful!'

'One shadow more!' said the ghost.

'No more!' cried Scrooge. 'I don't wish to see any more!' But the spirit held his arms, and he could not escape.

Now they were in another place, in a room which was not very large, but comfortable. Near the fire sat a beautiful young girl. Scrooge thought she was the girl that he had just seen, until he saw *her*, now a good-looking married lady, sitting opposite her daughter. The room was full of children, and noise, and shouting, and laughing. Just then the door opened, and the father entered, carrying a great

The father entered, carrying a great pile of Christmas presents.

pile of Christmas presents. The noise became twice as loud, as the children received their presents with delight, and kissed their father gratefully. Finally, the younger ones went upstairs to bed, and Scrooge watched more sadly than ever, as the father sat down with his loving daughter and her mother by the fire.

'Belle,' said the husband, turning to his wife with a smile, 'I saw an old friend of yours this afternoon. Guess who? Mr Scrooge! He was sitting alone in his office. His partner is dying, and I don't think he has any other friends.'

'Spirit!' said Scrooge in a broken voice. 'Take me away from this place.'

'These are shadows of the things that happened in the past,' said the ghost. 'You chose the life that you preferred, so why cry now?'

'I can't watch any more! It's too awful! Leave me alone, spirit!' And Scrooge, noticing that the ghostly light was burning high and bright, suddenly took the extinguisher, and pushed it down hard on the spirit's head. But although it covered the ghost's head and body, Scrooge could not hide the light, which continued to shine out strongly from underneath.

Now Scrooge found himself back in his own bedroom again. Feeling very tired, he climbed into bed and at once fell into a deep, heavy sleep.

3

The second of the three spirits

When Scrooge woke up, he realized immediately that the church clock was just going to strike one. He felt sure that the second spirit would soon visit him. This time he wanted to be ready, so he pulled back all the curtains round his bed himself, and lay there, waiting. At one o'clock, instead of a spirit, a strong light shone down on Scrooge's bed. He felt very frightened. After a few minutes he thought that perhaps the light was coming from the next room, so he got up and went to the door. When he touched it, a strange voice called his name, and asked him to enter. He obeyed.

Although he recognized it as his own room, it looked very different now. The walls were covered with bright green leaves, and there was a good fire burning in the fireplace. On the floor were big piles of the best Christmas food – wonderful rich dark cakes, warm soft bread, colourful apples and oranges, plates of yellow butter, cooked chickens, boxes of chocolates and sugared sweets. Sitting beside all this was a large, smiling spirit, who called out cheerfully to Scrooge, 'Come in! Come in, man! I am the ghost of Christmas Present! Look at me!'

Since the first ghost's visit, Scrooge was no longer very sure of himself. So although the spirit's eyes were clear and kind, Scrooge was afraid to look straight into its face. But he could see that its body was dressed in a long green robe, its long brown hair fell freely down its back, and its face wore a warm and friendly smile. Light shone from the torch which it was holding in its strong right hand.

'Spirit,' said Scrooge quietly, 'take me where you want. Last night I learned a lesson which is working now. If you have anything to teach me tonight, let me learn from you.'

'Touch my robe!' said the spirit, and Scrooge obeyed.

The food, the room, the fire all disappeared, and they were standing outside in the cold, snowy streets on Christmas morning. Although the sky was grey and the streets were dirty, the people looked surprisingly cheerful, as they hurried to the bakers' shops with their Christmas dinners, all ready for cooking. The spirit seemed specially interested in poor people. He stood with Scrooge in a baker's doorway and held his torch over the dinners as they were carried past him. Sometimes, when he saw people pushing each other or getting angry, he lifted his torch over their heads, and immediately they became kinder, or stopped arguing, 'because it's Christmas,' they told each other.

'What does your torch do, spirit?' asked Scrooge.

'It gives a special taste to people's dinners on this day,' answered the spirit.

'I am the ghost of Christmas Present!'

'Why do you use it most on poor people?' said Scrooge.

'Because poor people need it most,' was the reply.

They went on through London, and came to the small house where Scrooge's clerk lived. Here the spirit smiled, and held his torch high over the door. Inside, Bob Cratchit's wife and second daughter, Belinda, in their everyday dresses, but looking clean and pretty, were putting plates on the table for their Christmas dinner. Bob's son Peter was helping to cook the potatoes, and two smaller Cratchits, a boy and a girl, were running round excitedly. Just then the eldest daughter, Martha, arrived home from work.

'Here's Martha, mother!' cried the two young Cratchits happily. 'We're having a really big chicken for dinner, Martha!' In fact it was only a small chicken, but it seemed large to the excited children.

'My dear, how late you are!' said Mrs Cratchit, kissing her daughter several times.

'We were so busy yesterday, mother!' replied the girl. 'That's why we didn't finish until this morning!'

'Well! Never mind, now that you're here. God bless you! Sit down by the fire, my dear!'

'No, no! Father's coming!' cried the two young Cratchits. 'Hide, Martha, hide!'

So Martha hid herself, and in came Bob in his thin coat and long white scarf, with his son Tiny Tim in his arms. Poor Tiny Tim! He had not walked since he was born, and although he could pull himself and his thin little legs

29

along with the help of a wooden crutch, he was not strong enough to travel far alone.

'Why, where's Martha?' cried Bob, looking round.

'Not coming,' said Mrs Cratchit.

'Not coming!' repeated Bob, his cheerful smile disappearing. 'Not coming on Christmas Day!'

But Martha didn't like to worry her father for a minute, so she ran out from behind the door and kissed him, while the two young Cratchits showed Tiny Tim the chicken, now ready to eat.

Scrooge and the spirit watched as the family sat down to eat. It was a poor enough meal, but to them it seemed

wonderful, and they ate every bit of it.

'It's the best chicken *I've* ever tasted,' said Bob, smiling round at his family, who, with their mouths full, all agreed.

And then, the most exciting moment of the day! Belinda put a clean plate in front of each person, and they all turned to look at Mrs Cratchit as she came in from the kitchen. Her face was hot from her morning's work, but she was smiling happily as she carried in – the Christmas pudding, in its little circle of blue fire!

Oh, it was a wonderful pudding! They were all delighted with it.

'It's your greatest success in all the years that we've been

Oh, it was a wonderful pudding!

31

married, my dear!' said Bob.

'Well, I did wonder how much fruit to put in it,' said his wife, 'but, yes, it's a good one!' And she laughed just like a young girl.

Nobody said that it was a very small pudding for a large family. Nobody even *thought* it. No Cratchit ever said or thought things like that.

At last, when they had finished their meal, the children cleared the table and washed the plates. Then they all sat round the fire, eating apples and oranges. There was a large bowl of fruit and sugar and hot water and something a little stronger, but only three people could drink at the same time, because the family only owned two glasses and a cup. But this did not worry the Cratchits at all. Now Bob lifted his glass and said, 'A merry Christmas to us all, my dears! God bless us!'

The family repeated his wish, and Tiny Tim said, last of all, 'God bless us every one!' He sat very close to his father, on a small chair. Bob held his son's thin little hand in his own. The boy had a special place in his father's heart.

'Spirit,' said Scrooge, with an interest that he had never felt before, 'tell me if Tiny Tim will live.'

'In the future I see an empty chair by the fire, with a crutch beside it. If these shadows do not change, the child will die.'

'No, no!' said Scrooge. 'Oh no, kind spirit ! Say that he will live!'

'If his life does not change soon, he will die before next

Christmas. What does that matter? There are too many people in the world, so it's a good thing if some of them die.'

Scrooge was ashamed and sad to hear his own words spoken by the spirit. But he lifted his head when he heard his name.

'Mr Scrooge!' said Bob. 'Let's drink to Mr Scrooge, whose money has paid for this meal!'

'His money!' said Mrs Cratchit angrily. 'What can we buy with his fifteen shillings a week? Why should we drink to the health of a hateful, hard, unfeeling, mean old man like Scrooge?'

'My dear,' said Bob gently, 'remember it's Christmas.'

'Well, Bob, I'll drink to his health only because of you and because it's Christmas. Long life to Mr Scrooge! A merry Christmas and a happy new year to him! He'll be very merry and very happy, I'm sure!'

When the children heard Scrooge's name, a dark shadow came over their happiness for a while, and they were quiet and a little sad. But five minutes later they were talking, and laughing, and telling stories, ten times merrier than before. They were not a good-looking or a well-dressed family, but they were happy and grateful and loved each other. As they disappeared in the light of the spirit's torch, Scrooge could not take his eyes off them, especially Tiny Tim.

By this time it was getting dark, and snowing heavily. The spirit took Scrooge into many houses, where fires were burning cheerfully, and food was cooking, and people were

33

merrily welcoming their friends and families into their homes. The ghost was delighted to see all this excitement, and made sure that he lifted his torch over every poor family, to give them more fun, and better food, and greater happiness.

Then the spirit took Scrooge away from the busy capital, to a wild, lonely place in the country, where no trees grew. Here they visited a small stone house, a long way from any town or village, where an old man and woman were singing Christmas carols, with their children and grandchildren. The spirit did not stay long here, but told Scrooge to hold his robe again.

'Where are we going? Not up in the air, surely!' And Scrooge, terribly frightened, looked down as they flew over the land and then over the sea. It was stormy, windy weather, and the waves crashed violently underneath them. The spirit took Scrooge to a lighthouse built on a lonely rock, several miles from land. A light was kept burning at the top, in order to warn sailors to keep away from the dangerous rocks. Two men lived here in this cold, unfriendly place, far away from their families, but the spirit smiled to see them shake hands, wish each other a merry Christmas, and sing a carol together in front of their fire.

Again the spirit and Scrooge flew on, and together they landed on a ship in the middle of the sea. Here every man, although many miles from home, had a kind word for his friend, or thought warmly of his family, because it was Christmas.

34

The two men wished each other a merry Christmas.

It was a great surprise to Scrooge, while listening to the noise of the wind and waves, to hear a happy laugh. He recognized it as his nephew's, and found himself, with the smiling spirit beside him, in his nephew's bright, warm sitting-room.

When Scrooge's nephew laughed, everybody who was with him wanted to laugh too. He had that kind of laugh. And at the moment, his very pretty wife and several of his friends were laughing with him.

'He said that Christmas was humbug! Ha ha ha!' cried Scrooge's nephew.

'That's very bad of him, Fred!' said his wife.

'He's a strange old man,' said Scrooge's nephew, 'but I'm sorry for him. His money is no use to him, you see. He isn't at all happy or comfortable, although he's rich. It's sad to think of him sitting alone in his cold room. And so I'm going to invite him every Christmas. He can be cross and miserable if he likes, but I'll go on inviting him and one day perhaps he'll think better of Christmas!'

After tea, the cheerful little group sang songs, and played music. Scrooge recognized the song that his little sister used to sing, and remembered sadly what the ghost of Christmas Past had shown him. Later the friends played guessing games, and Scrooge joined in the games with delight. Nobody except the spirit could hear him, but he often guessed the right answer.

'It's time to go now,' said the ghost, smiling at the old man's childish excitement.

'No, spirit, please, let me stay a little longer. Look, they're playing a new game!'

It was a game called Yes and No, in which Scrooge's nephew had to think of something, and the others had to ask questions to discover what it was. The only possible answers were Yes or No. Scrooge heard that Fred was thinking of a living animal, a wild animal, sometimes an angry animal, which lived in London and walked in the streets. Every time he answered a question, Fred could not stop himself laughing. At last, his wife's dark, pretty sister started laughing too.

'I know what it is, Fred! I know!' she cried out. 'It's your uncle Scro–o–o–o–oge!'

Everyone laughed until they cried. What a wonderful game! What a clever idea of Fred's! But at last Fred dried his eyes, and said, 'We've been very merry because of him, so I think we should drink to his health. Here's to Uncle Scrooge! A merry Christmas and a happy new year to the old man! Uncle Scrooge!'

'To Uncle Scrooge!' they all cried, cheerfully lifting their glasses.

Uncle Scrooge wanted to thank them, but the spirit hurried him away. The ghost seemed much older now: his brown hair had become grey.

'Are spirits' lives so short?' asked Scrooge.

'My life in this world ends at midnight tonight. Listen! It's a quarter to midnight now!'

The church clock was striking the three quarters.

'Excuse me for asking, spirit,' said Scrooge, 'but what are those strange things near your foot?'

'Oh man, look here!' said the spirit sadly, and brought out from under his robe two ghostly figures, a boy and a girl. They were thin and poorly dressed, with cold, mean eyes and dry, yellow skin, and their faces showed only a frightening and murderous hate. Scrooge had never seen anything so terrible or so sad.

'These miserable children are Man's,' said the spirit.

'These miserable children are Man's,' said the spirit. 'The boy is Crime. The girl is Need. They will destroy Man if nothing is done about them.'

'Can't anyone help them?' cried Scrooge.

'Are there no prisons?' said the spirit, turning on Scrooge for the last time with his own words. 'Are there no workhouses?'

The clock struck twelve. Scrooge looked, but could no longer see the ghost or the children. He was alone again.

4
The last of the spirits

'The third spirit will come at midnight.' Scrooge suddenly remembered the words of Jacob Marley's ghost, and, lifting his eyes, saw a spirit, all in black, coming slowly towards him. It was a tall, silent figure, wearing a long black robe which hid its head and body. When it came close to him, it stopped and pointed onwards with one hand. Scrooge was more afraid of this spirit than he had been of the others, and his voice was shaking as he asked, 'Are you the spirit of Christmas Yet to Come?' The ghost neither spoke nor moved, but still pointed onwards.

'Are you going to show me shadows of the things which haven't happened yet, but will happen in the future?' Scrooge asked.

There was no answer.

'Ghost of the future!' he continued. 'You frighten me very much, but I think you can help me to change my life. I'll be very grateful to you if you show me the future. Won't you speak to me?'

Again, no reply.

'Well, show me the way, spirit!' said Scrooge finally.

'The night is passing, and time is valuable to me, I know.'

The ghost moved away, with Scrooge following in its shadow. Suddenly they were in the heart of the capital, among the businessmen and moneylenders. The ghost pointed to one small group of men, so Scrooge went closer to listen to their conversation.

'No, I don't know much about it,' said one fat man. 'I only know he's dead.'

'When did he die?' asked another man.

'Last night, I think.'

'Why, what was the matter with him?' asked a third.

'I've no idea,' replied the fat man, looking bored. 'Who cares?'

'What's he done with his money?' asked a red-faced gentleman.

'I haven't heard,' said the fat man. 'He hasn't left it to me, that's all I know.'

They all laughed at this. Scrooge knew the men, and looked towards the spirit, hoping it would explain what the conversation meant. But the ghost moved on, pointing at two more men. Scrooge listened again. He knew these men well. They were rich and important, and he had often done business with them.

'How are you?' said one.

'How are *you*?' replied the other.

'Well!' said the first. 'The old man has died at last, has he?'

'So they tell me,' replied the second. 'Cold, isn't it?'

'He hasn't left his money to me,' said the fat man.

'Nice and frosty for Christmas. Good morning!'

Not another word. That was the end of their meeting.

Scrooge wondered why the spirit wanted him to hear these conversations. What could they mean? The dead man could not be his partner Jacob, because *he* was already dead. Scrooge watched carefully, trying to understand. He looked round for his own shadow, but could not see himself anywhere. 'Perhaps that's not surprising,' he thought, 'because if I change my life, and I'm planning to do that, I won't be the same person in the future!' Just then he noticed the spirit, standing quiet and dark beside him, with its pointing hand. He felt the unseen eyes staring fixedly at him behind the black robe. Scrooge's body shook, and he felt cold.

They left the busy offices and banks, and went to another part of the capital, where Scrooge had never been before.

The streets were narrow and dirty, the houses miserably poor, the people unwashed and half-dressed. Down one street there was a small shop, where an old man was sitting waiting for customers. His business was buying old furniture or clothes, and selling them again, to the poorest people in London. As Scrooge and the spirit watched, three women arrived at the shop door at the same time, each carrying a large bundle. They looked very surprised and a little ashamed to see each other. Suddenly they all started laughing.

'Ladies, you couldn't find a better place to meet,' said Joe, the old man, getting up. 'Now come inside, and show me what you've got to sell.'

Inside, the first woman put her bundle on the table and said, 'I don't care if everybody knows where this comes from! We all have to take care of ourselves! *He* always did!'

'Now what have we here?' said old Joe,
opening the bundles.

'That's right,' agreed the second woman.

'Very true,' agreed the third.

'Does a dead man need these things?' continued the first woman. 'And why was he so mean while he was alive? We all worked for him, didn't we? Cleaned his house, washed his clothes, cooked his soup? And what did we get? Three shillings a week! It's no surprise that he died alone, with no friends around him!'

'You never spoke a truer word,' said the second.

'He was a bad man, we all know that,' said the third.

'Now what have we here?' said old Joe, opening the women's bundles. 'Buttons, pencils, boots, silver spoons, some excellent bed-curtains, blankets and – a very good shirt,' he added, feeling the fine cotton.

'Yes, it was his best,' said the first woman. 'They put it on him after he died. But he doesn't need it now that he's dead! And the blankets and bed-curtains! He doesn't need them either!'

'You took the shirt off a dead body, and the blankets and curtains off his bed, while he was lying there! Well, well!' said Joe, shaking his head. 'Here's your money.' And he counted out several shillings into the women's hands.

'Ha ha ha!' laughed the first woman. 'He frightened everyone away when he was alive, and we've made money out of him now that he's dead! Ha ha ha!'

Scrooge felt sick and angry at the same time. 'Spirit,' he said, 'I see now. *I* could be that unhappy man. Good Heavens, what's this?'

Joe and the women had disappeared, and Scrooge was standing in a dark room. Opposite him was a bed, with no blankets or curtains. A light shone down from above, on to the body of a dead man, covered with a sheet.

'How sad,' thought Scrooge, 'to die with no friends or family around him! To lie in an empty room, with no candles or flowers, and robbed of his clothes! To know that nobody loves him, because he loved nobody in his life! Money can't buy a happy life, or a peaceful death!' He looked at the spirit, whose hand was pointing at the man's covered head. It would be easy to lift the sheet, and see who the man was. But for some reason Scrooge could not do it.

'Spirit,' he said, 'this is a terrible place. Let's go!'

Still the ghost's unmoving finger pointed at the man's head.

'I understand you, but I can't look at him, spirit, I can't!' said Scrooge wildly. 'If there's anyone in this town who feels anything at this man's death, show that person to me, spirit, please!'

For a moment the spirit lifted its dark robe like a wing, and showed Scrooge a room, where a mother and her children were sitting. The young woman kept looking at the clock, and when her husband arrived, she hurried to meet him.

'What – what is the news?' she asked him worriedly. 'Is it good . . . or . . . or bad?'

'There is still hope, Caroline,' he replied.

'How can there be hope? If that hard, mean old man wants us to pay back the money now, they'll send us to prison! We haven't got enough to pay him!'

'He is dead, Caroline,' answered her husband.

'Thank God for that!' cried the young woman from her heart. The next moment she realized what she had said. 'Oh, I didn't mean that. I'm sorry if *anyone* dies.'

'Perhaps the person who inherits his business will give us more time to pay the money back. And we'll have the money by then. Tonight we can sleep well, Caroline!'

'So, spirit,' said Scrooge in a broken voice, 'you can show me only happiness at this man's death. It frightens me, spirit. Show me, please, that there *can* be sadness at a death.'

The ghost took him silently through the streets, to poor Bob Cratchit's house. The room seemed strangely quiet.

The mother and her daughters were making a small white cotton shirt together, while the usually noisy young Cratchits sat silently in a corner, and Peter was reading a book. Mrs Cratchit put her work down on the table, and covered her face with her hand.

'The colour hurts my eyes,' she said. The colour? Ah, poor Tiny Tim!

'They're a little better now,' she went on. 'It's difficult to work by candlelight. And I don't want to show red eyes to your father when he comes home.'

'He's a bit late,' said Peter, 'but I think he's walked more slowly these last few days, mother.'

They were very quiet again. At last she said bravely, 'I've known him walk with – with Tiny Tim in his arms, very fast indeed.'

'So have I,' cried Peter. 'Often!'

'But he was very light to carry, and your father loved him so much! And there's your father at the door now!' She got up quickly to kiss Bob as he came in. He looked tired and thin, and needed his long scarf, poor man! Martha took his boots and scarf off, and Belinda brought him his tea, and the little Cratchits sat close to him. He was very cheerful with all of them, and was pleased with the little shirt that his wife and daughters were making.

'It'll be ready long before Sunday, won't it?' he said.

'Sunday! You went there today, then, Bob?' asked his wife.

'Yes, my dear. You'd love to see it. It's a beautiful green

place. But you'll see it often. I promised him that we would go there every Sunday. My little, little child!' cried Bob, hiding his face in his hands. He had loved the boy very much.

He went upstairs to the quiet bedroom, where the child lay. Poor Bob sat down beside him, and when he felt calmer, he kissed the little face, and went downstairs again, almost happy.

'My dears,' he said to his children, 'one of these days some of you will marry and leave home. In a few years' time perhaps all of you will. But I'm sure none of us will ever forget Tiny Tim, will we?'

'Never, father!' they all cried.

'And I know,' said Bob, 'that when we remember how patient and gentle he was, although he was only a little child, we won't argue among ourselves. We'll remember

'My little, little child!' cried Bob.

poor Tiny Tim, and love each other!'

'We will, father!' they all cried again.

'I am very happy,' said Bob. 'I am very happy!' Mrs Cratchit kissed him, his daughters kissed him, the two young Cratchits kissed him, and he and Peter shook hands. Tiny Tim, your goodness lives on in your family!

'Spirit,' said Scrooge, 'I know that you will leave me soon. Tell me who that dead man on the bed was!'

No answer came in words, but the ghost of Christmas Yet to Come took Scrooge through the streets of London again.

'Wait a moment,' said Scrooge. 'We're passing my office. Let me see how I shall look in the future!'

The spirit stopped. Its hand was pointing away from the office. But Scrooge hurried up to the window and looked in. It was an office still, but not his. The furniture was not the same, and the figure in the chair was not himself. The ghost continued to point onwards, and Scrooge followed. They reached a church, and entered the churchyard. Here, among the untidy graves and the uncut grass, lay the miserable man whose name Scrooge would soon learn. It was a lonely place, most suitable for a man so unloved.

The spirit stood and pointed down at one of the graves. Scrooge was strangely afraid.

'Before I look more closely at that gravestone,' he said, 'answer me one question. Are these the shadows of the things that *will* be, or are they only shadows of the things that *may* be?'

The spirit pointed down at one of the graves.

Without replying, the ghost pointed silently down at the grave. Scrooge moved slowly towards it, and following the finger, read on the stone his own name, EBENEZER SCROOGE.

'Am *I* that man who was lying on the bed?' he cried.

49

The spirit pointed from the grave to him, and back again.
'No, spirit! Oh, no, no!'
The finger was still there.

Scrooge fell to the ground in front of the ghost, holding its long dark robe. 'Spirit! Listen! I am a changed man! I have learnt my lesson from you spirits! Why show me this terrible end, if there is no hope for me!'

For the first time the hand appeared to shake.

'Good spirit, tell me that my future will change, if I change my life now!'

The kind hand shook again.

'I will remember the past, and think of the future. I will be good to other people. I will keep Christmas in my heart, and will try to be kind, and cheerful, and merry, every day. Oh, tell me I can clean away the writing on this stone!'

Suddenly it became –
a bedpost.

Wildly, he caught the ghostly hand and held it for a moment. But the spirit was stronger than him, and pulled its hand away. Just then Scrooge noticed that something strange was happening to the spirit. It was getting smaller and smaller, and suddenly it became – a bedpost.

5

The end of the story

_Y_es! and the bedpost was his own. The bed was his own, the room was his own. Best and happiest of all, the future was his own, to change his life in!

'I will remember the past, and think of the future,' repeated Scrooge, as he jumped out of bed. 'God bless you, Jacob Marley! And God bless Christmas!'

In his excitement he found it difficult to speak. His face was still wet from crying. 'Here are my bed-curtains!' he cried delightedly. 'They aren't stolen! And I'm alive! Those were only shadows of things that _may_ be! The future will be different! I know it will!'

All this time his hands were busy, hurriedly putting on his clothes. He put his left foot in his right shoe, couldn't find the buttons on his shirt, and forgot to brush his hair.

'I don't know what I'm doing!' said Scrooge, laughing and crying at the same time. 'A merry Christmas to everybody! A happy new year to all the world! Hurrah! There's the door which Jacob's ghost came through! There's the corner where the ghost of Christmas Present sat! There's

'I don't know what I'm doing!' said Scrooge.

the window where I saw the travelling ghosts! It's all true, it all happened! Ha ha ha!'

Really, for a man who hadn't laughed for so many years, it was an excellent laugh. The father of a long line of excellent laughs!

'I don't know what day of the month it is!' said Scrooge. 'I don't know how long I've been with the spirits! I don't know anything. I'm just like a baby. Never mind! I prefer being a baby! Hurrah!'

Just then he heard the church bells ring out louder than he had ever heard before. Running to the window, he opened it and looked out. No fog at all, a clear, bright, cold day, golden sunlight, blue sky, sweet clean air, merry bells. Oh, wonderful! Wonderful!

'What's today?' he cried, calling down to a boy in the street.

'Today?' replied the boy, in great surprise. 'Why, it's *Christmas Day*!'

'So I haven't missed it!' thought Scrooge. 'The spirits have done it all in one night!' He called down to the boy again, 'Hallo, young man! Do you know the meat shop at the corner of the next street?'

'Of course I do,' replied the boy.

'What an intelligent boy!' said Scrooge. 'Do you know if they've sold the big turkey that was in the shop window yesterday?'

'What, the one as big as me?' asked the boy.

'What a delightful boy!' said Scrooge. 'It's wonderful talking to him. Yes, that's the one!'

'It's still there in the window,' said the boy.

'Is it?' said Scrooge. 'Well, go and buy it.'

'You don't mean it!' cried the boy.

'I do, I do. I'm serious. Go and buy it, and tell the man to bring it back here. Come back with the man and I'll give you a shilling. Come back in less than five minutes and I'll give you three shillings!'

The boy went off like a bullet from a gun.

'I'll send the turkey to Bob Cratchit's!' laughed Scrooge. 'He'll never know who's sent it! It's twice as big as Tiny Tim! Ha ha ha!'

He went on laughing as he wrote Bob's address, gave it to the man with the turkey, and paid for a taxi, because the turkey was much too heavy to carry all the way to Camden Town.

Now he finished dressing, and went out into the streets, wearing his best clothes. The town was full of happy, busy people, and Scrooge smiled at all of them. Three or four men said cheerfully to him, 'Good morning, sir! And a merry Christmas to you!' Scrooge thought these were the best sounds that he had ever heard.

As he was walking, he suddenly noticed one of the comfortable-looking gentlemen who had come to his office to ask for money for the poor. Scrooge went straight up to him, took the old gentleman by both hands, and said, 'My dear sir, how are you? A merry Christmas to you, sir!'

'Mr Scrooge?' asked the gentleman, surprised.

'Yes, that's my name. I'm very sorry for what I said to you when you visited me yesterday. Will you please—' and he spoke very quietly in the gentleman's ear.

'Good Heavens!' cried the gentleman. 'My dear Mr Scrooge, are you serious?'

'I am. Not a shilling less. I must tell you, I haven't given anything to anyone for years.'

'My dear sir!' said the gentleman, shaking hands with him. 'I don't know how to thank you for—'

'Don't say anything, please,' replied Scrooge. 'Will you come and see me tomorrow about it?'

'I will!' cried the old gentleman happily.

He gave Bob's address to the man with the turkey.

'Thank you, and God bless you!' said Scrooge.

He went to church, and watched the people, and gave children money for sweets, and discovered that he had never been so happy in his life. In the afternoon he went to his nephew's house. He passed the door several times before he was brave enough to knock. But at last he did it, and was taken into the sitting-room, where Fred and his pretty wife were waiting for their friends to arrive for dinner.

'Fred!' said Scrooge. 'It's your uncle Scrooge. I've come to dinner. Will you let me stay, Fred?'

Let him stay! Fred almost shook his uncle's arm off. Scrooge felt at home in five minutes. Nothing could be merrier. And what a wonderful dinner they had! Wonderful party, wonderful games, wonderful happiness!

But he was early at the office next morning. Oh, he was there early. He wanted to catch Bob Cratchit arriving late. And he did! The clock struck nine. No Bob. A quarter past. No Bob. He was eighteen and a half minutes late when he finally hurried in. Scrooge was sitting with his office door open.

'Hallo!' said Scrooge in his old, hard voice. 'What do you mean by coming here so late?'

'I'm very sorry, sir,' said Bob. 'I *am* late. It's only once a year. We were rather merry yesterday, sir.'

'Now I'll tell you what, my friend,' said Scrooge, 'I'm not going to have this any longer. And so,' he continued, jumping off his chair and shaking Bob's hand, 'I'm going to pay you twice as much!'

Bob's face went white. For a second or two he thought that Scrooge had gone crazy.

'A merry Christmas, Bob!' said Scrooge, and it was clear that he meant it. 'A merrier Christmas, Bob, than I've given you for a long time. I'm going to pay you well, and help you with your family, and we'll discuss it all this afternoon over a Christmas drink, Bob! Put more wood on the fire at once, Bob Cratchit, and let's be comfortable!'

Scrooge did everything that he had promised, and more. To Tiny Tim, who did NOT die, he became a second father. He became as good a friend, employer and man, as anyone in London or in the world. Some people laughed to see the change in him, but he did not care. His own heart laughed inside him, and that was good enough for him.

'A merry Christmas, Bob!' said Scrooge.

He never had any more conversations with spirits, but kept Christmas cheerfully, and lived a happy life. That is what all of us want, and so, as Tiny Tim said, 'God bless us, every one!'

GLOSSARY

carol a special song which people sing at Christmas

cheerful looking or sounding happy

Christmas Eve 24th December, the day before Christmas Day

clerk someone who works in an office, writing letters, etc.

delight a pleased and happy feeling

delighted very pleased and happy

extinguisher a thing shaped like a tall hat, which you put on a candle to stop it burning

fog a thick mist that stops you seeing clearly

foggy very misty

frost a thin white cover of ice on the ground in very cold weather; (on page 2, Scrooge's white hair and cold heart)

God bless you! people used to say this when they liked someone or were grateful to them

humbug nonsense, silly ideas; dishonest or untrue words

kiss *(v)* to touch someone lovingly with your lips

merry happy, cheerful

partner someone who owns a business with another person

point *(v)* to show with your finger or arm where something is

present *(n)* the time now (not past, not future)

shilling a coin in old British money (equal to five pence today)

spirit the ghost of a dead person, or a kind of 'person' without a living body

stare to look hard at something or someone for a long time

strike (past tense **struck**) (of a clock) to tell the hour, half hour, or quarter hour by sounding a bell

tiny very small

A Christmas Carol

ACTIVITIES

Before Reading

1 The title of this story is *A Christmas Carol*. Do you think it is going to be about . . .

   1 Christmas music?   ③ changes in someone's life?
   2 a party in winter?   4 a baby girl?

2 Read the story introduction on the first page of the book, and the back cover. What have you found out? Cross out the words that are wrong.

   1 Scrooge is a *kind/cross*, *miserable/happy*, *mean/generous* old man, who *enjoys/hates* Christmas and is only interested in *family life/making money*.
   2 Bob Cratchit is Scrooge's *clerk/partner* and he works in a *warm/cold office/library* with a *small/large* fire.
   3 Jacob Marley, Scrooge's *clerk/partner*, is *dead/alive*.
   4 *Frightening/Enjoyable* things happen to Scrooge on Christmas *Day/Eve*, and he sees *three/four* ghosts.
   5 By Christmas Day, Scrooge *is a changed man / has forgotten all about it*.

3 How much do you know about Christmas in Britain? Think about these questions.

   1 Do people give presents?
   2 What kind of food do people eat?

3 Do people go to work, or to church, or stay at home?
4 Do people visit friends or family?
5 What do people say when they meet in the street?

What do you do in your country for special holidays like Christmas?

4 **This is a ghost story. What do you think about ghosts?**

1 What time of day or night do ghosts usually appear?
2 Are ghosts always frightening?
3 What do you expect a ghost to look like?
4 What kinds of message do ghosts often bring?
5 Do you believe in ghosts?
6 Have you ever seen a ghost?
7 Do you know anyone who has seen a ghost?

5 **'Scrooge learns a lesson that he will never forget.' Can you guess what kind of lesson? Choose Y (Yes), N (No) or P (Perhaps) for each of these ideas.**

1 He loses all his money. Y/N/P
2 He dies of heart trouble. Y/N/P
3 His family refuses to speak to him. Y/N/P
4 He finds the love of his life again. Y/N/P
5 He has no one to work for him. Y/N/P
6 He sees what the future holds for him. Y/N/P
7 He learns to like people. Y/N/P
8 He has his tongue cut out. Y/N/P

ACTIVITIES

While Reading

Read Chapter 1. Who said this, and to whom? What, or who, were they talking about?

1 'You're too rich to be unhappy.'
2 'I'll see you dead first!'
3 'Many can't go there, and many prefer to die.'
4 'It's only once a year, sir.'
5 'I am here tonight to warn you.'

Read Chapter 2. Here are some untrue sentences. Rewrite them with the correct information.

1 Nothing happened when the clock struck one.
2 The ghost took Scrooge back to his past, but Scrooge did not remember any of it.
3 Scrooge's eyes were wet because he had a cold.
4 Old Fezziwig made his clerks work on Christmas Eve.
5 Scrooge had never wanted to marry anybody.

Read Chapter 3. Choose the best question-word for these questions, and then answer them.

Who / Where / Why

1 ... did the ghost of Christmas Present take Scrooge first?
2 ... did the spirit hold his torch over people's heads?
3 ... had a special place in Bob Cratchit's heart?

62

4 . . . didn't Mrs Cratchit want to drink to Scrooge's health?
5 . . . played a Yes/No game?
6 . . . were the ghostly figures under the ghost's robe?

Read Chapter 4, and then match these halves of sentences.

1 Scrooge was more afraid of the last of the spirits than . . .
2 The spirit showed him shadows of things which hadn't happened yet, but . . .
3 From the businessmen's conversations Scrooge learnt . . .
4 The three women sold Scrooge's clothes because . . .
5 A young family had to pay some money to Scrooge so . . .
6 When Scrooge wanted to see sadness at a death, . . .
7 In the churchyard, the ghost pointed at a grave which . . .
8 they were happy to hear of his death.
9 would happen in the future.
10 the ghost showed him the Cratchits after Tiny Tim died.
11 he had been of the others.
12 had Scrooge's name on the gravestone.
13 he had paid them very badly when he was alive.
14 that nobody cared about the man who had died.

Before you read Chapter 5, can you guess the answers to these questions?

1 Will Scrooge keep his promises to the spirit?
2 Will the spirits appear to him again?
3 Will Tiny Tim die?
4 Where will Scrooge go on Christmas Day?

After Reading

1 **On the day after Christmas, what did Bob Cratchit tell his wife when he went home after work? Choose the best words to complete their conversation (one word for each gap.)**

WIFE: You're home _____, Bob! It's only three o'clock! What's happened? Was Mr Scrooge _____ because you were _____ this morning?

BOB: No, not at all. In fact, he _____ my hand and wished me a _____ Christmas!

WIFE: But Mr Scrooge never says that. He _____ Christmas!

BOB: I know. At first I thought he had gone _____! He always used to say that Christmas was _____. He was always _____ and cross, but now he's happy and _____.

WIFE: But why has he _____, Bob?

BOB: He said that he learnt a _____ last night that he will never _____. I don't know what happened to him, but I do know that he sent the big _____ that arrived yesterday!

WIFE: Mr Scrooge _____ for our Christmas dinner? Oh my!

BOB: But the _____ news is this, my dear. He's going to pay me thirty _____ a week instead of fifteen!

WIFE: But that's _____ as much! Oh my, oh my!

BOB: And he wants to _____ us with the family, and be a second _____ to Tiny Tim.

WIFE: Oh my, oh my, oh my! Well, God _____ Mr Scrooge!

2 **Match the characters' names with their descriptions.**

Bob Cratchit	Belle
Ebenezer Scrooge	Mr Fezziwig
Scrooge's nephew, Fred	Tiny Tim
Scrooge's sister	Jacob Marley
Ghost of Christmas Past	
Ghost of Christmas Present	
Ghost of Christmas Yet to Come	

- A large, kind-looking old gentleman
- A tall, silent figure in a black robe
- A little boy who could not walk
- A young man with a happy laugh
- A clerk with a long white scarf
- A spirit who had been unable to rest for seven years
- A figure with long brown hair and a warm, friendly smile
- An old man with red eyes, white hair, and a cross voice
- A warm-hearted little girl
- A beautiful young girl who loved a cold-hearted man
- A figure with long white hair, but soft, young skin

3 **Which of these characters belong to Scrooge's past life, and which to his present life? Make two lists.**

Dick Wilkins	Belle
Jacob Marley	Fred
Tiny Tim	Bob Cratchit
Scrooge's sister	Mr and Mrs Fezziwig

4 Perhaps Scrooge's sister sent a letter to her son, Fred, just before she died. Put the sentences in the right order to make her letter.

My dear Fred,

1 Before I die, there's one thing I want to ask you – try to be a good friend to your uncle Ebenezer.

2 Take care of yourself, my dear boy, and think of me sometimes, when I am gone.

3 I don't think I have long left to live now, so this will probably be my last letter to you.

4 You see, our father was a cold, hard man, who didn't love Ebenezer at all.

5 But when she realized that he would always love money more than her, she married another man.

6 When he was older and started work, he began to show an unhealthy interest in money, and that was the reason why he never married.

7 I know he seems to hate people, but remember that he had a difficult life when he was younger.

8 Poor Ebenezer! I know that you, with your warm heart, will feel sorry for him, now that I've told you this.

9 And so, as a child, Ebenezer too became cold, and spent a lot of time alone.

10 There *was* a girl who loved him once, a beautiful young woman called Belle.

Your loving mother

5 **What is the message of this story? Complete the sentences to explain your ideas.**

1 You should always try _____

2 Nobody likes _____

3 The most important thing in life is _____

4 It is never too late _____

6 **What do you think about this story? Can people really change that easily? Complete this passage to make a different ending for the story. (Use as many words as you like.)**

Ebenezer Scrooge did not do everything that _____. He did pay Bob Cratchit thirty shillings a year, but poor Bob had to _____. It was too late for Scrooge to _____, and soon he became as _____. There was no extra wood _____, and Scrooge never became _____. Sadly, Tiny Tim _____. The Cratchit family were very unhappy, but they _____.

Scrooge's heart grew colder and colder, until one day he _____. Now he lies in the graveyard, in the cold, hard ground, and nobody _____.

7 **Here are some different titles for the story. Some are better than others. Can you say why?**

A Cheerful Man   Mr Ebenezer Scrooge

The Ghosts of Christmas Eve   Humbug!

Tiny Tim   Time to Change

Merry Christmas   The Wings of the Night

ABOUT THE AUTHOR

Charles John Huffam Dickens (1812–70) was born in Portsmouth, in England. His family were bad at managing their money, and they were very poor. The worst time for Dickens was when his father went to prison, because he could not pay back money he had borrowed, and Dickens was sent, aged only 12, to work in a factory. He remembered this terrible time all his life, and wrote about it in his novel *David Copperfield* twenty-five years later. He became a newspaper reporter, and wrote his first novel, *The Pickwick Papers* (1837), which was very popular. In the next four years, he wrote three more novels, *Oliver Twist*, *Nicholas Nickleby* and *The Old Curiosity Shop*, which were all very successful. People loved *A Christmas Carol*, when it appeared in 1843. In *A Tale of Two Cities*, a story about the French Revolution, he showed his interest in history, and in *Great Expectations*, he wrote about the differences between the rich and the poor, which he had known himself in his own early life.

He spent long hours at his writing desk, but he also had time for his large circle of family and friends, and for helping people. He thought that all people should be free, and have enough money to live a comfortable life. As he grew older, he worked harder than ever, giving public readings of his works in Britain and America, and continuing to write novels.

There have been hundreds of books, films and plays about Dickens' stories. Many people think he is the greatest English novelist of all time.

ABOUT BOOKWORMS

OXFORD BOOKWORMS LIBRARY
Classics • True Stories • Fantasy & Horror • Human Interest
Crime & Mystery • Thriller & Adventure

The OXFORD BOOKWORMS LIBRARY offers a wide range of original and adapted stories, both classic and modern, which take learners from elementary to advanced level through six carefully graded language stages:

Stage 1 (400 headwords)	**Stage 4** (1400 headwords)
Stage 2 (700 headwords)	**Stage 5** (1800 headwords)
Stage 3 (1000 headwords)	**Stage 6** (2500 headwords)

More than fifty titles are also available on cassette, and there are many titles at Stages 1 to 4 which are specially recommended for younger learners. In addition to the introductions and activities in each Bookworm, resource material includes photocopiable test worksheets and Teacher's Handbooks, which contain advice on running a class library and using cassettes, and the answers for the activities in the books.

Several other series are linked to the OXFORD BOOKWORMS LIBRARY. They range from highly illustrated readers for young learners, to playscripts, non-fiction readers, and unsimplified texts for advanced learners.

Oxford Bookworms Starters   *Oxford Bookworms Factfiles*
Oxford Bookworms Playscripts   *Oxford Bookworms Collection*

Details of these series and a full list of all titles in the OXFORD BOOKWORMS LIBRARY can be found in the *Oxford English* catalogues. A selection of titles from the OXFORD BOOKWORMS LIBRARY can be found on the next pages.

The Prisoner of Zenda

ANTHONY HOPE

Retold by Diane Mowat

'We must leave for Zenda at once, to find the King!' cried Sapt. 'If we're caught, we'll all be killed!'

So Rudolf Rassendyll and Sapt gallop through the night to find the King of Ruritania. But the King is now a prisoner in the Castle of Zenda. Who will rescue him from his enemies, the dangerous Duke Michael and Rupert of Hentzau?

And who will win the heart of the beautiful Princess Flavia?

Through the Looking-Glass

LEWIS CARROLL

Retold by Jennifer Bassett

'I wish I could get through into looking-glass house,' Alice said. 'Let's pretend that the glass has gone soft and . . . Why, I do believe it has! It's turning into a kind of cloud!'

A moment later Alice is inside the looking-glass world. There she finds herself part of a great game of chess, travelling through forests and jumping across brooks. The chess pieces talk and argue with her, give orders and repeat poems . . .

It is the strangest dream that anyone ever had . . .

Moondial

HELEN CRESSWELL

Retold by John Escott

'Moondial!' As Minty spoke the word, a cold wind went past her, and her ears were filled with a thousand frightened voices. She shut her eyes and put her hands over her ears – and the voices and the wind went away. Minty opened her eyes . . . *and knew that she was in a different morning, not the one she had woken up to.*

And so Minty's strange adventure begins – a journey through time into the past, where she finds Tom, and Sarah . . . and the evil Miss Vole.

Love Story

ERICH SEGAL

Retold by Rosemary Border

This is a love story you won't forget. Oliver Barrett meets Jenny Cavilleri. He plays sports, she plays music. He's rich, and she's poor. They argue, and they fight, and they fall in love.

So they get married, and make a home together. They work hard, they enjoy life, they make plans for the future. Then they learn that they don't have much time left.

Their story has made people laugh, and cry, all over the world.

Ethan Frome

EDITH WHARTON

Retold by Susan Kingsley

Life is always hard for the poor, in any place and at any time. Ethan Frome is a farmer in Massachusetts. He works long hours every day, but his farm makes very little money. His wife, Zeena, is a thin, grey woman, always complaining, and only interested in her own ill health.

Then Mattie Silver, a young cousin, comes to live with the Fromes, to help Zeena and do the housework. Her bright smile and laughing voice bring light and hope into the Fromes' house – and into Ethan's lonely life.

But poverty is a prison from which few people escape . . .

A Tale of Two Cities

CHARLES DICKENS

Retold by Ralph Mowat

'The Marquis lay there, like stone, with a knife pushed into his heart. On his chest lay a piece of paper, with the words: *Drive him fast to his grave. This is from JACQUES.*'

The French Revolution brings terror and death to many people. But even in these troubled times people can still love and be kind. They can be generous and true-hearted . . . and brave.